P9-APG-218

Loving Vows

Inspiring Promises for Building and Renewing Your Marriage

By
Barbara Eklof

Adams Media Corporation
Avon, Massachusetts

Dedication

To my adored family
Bill, Zelinda, and Carl

Copyright © 2002, Barbara Eklof. All rights reserved.
This book, or parts thereof, may not be reproduced
in any form without permission from the publisher;
exceptions are made for brief excerpts used in published reviews.

Published by Adams Media Corporation
57 Littlefield Street, Avon, MA 02322
www.adamsmedia.com

ISBN: 1-58062-571-1

Printed in Canada.

J I H G F E D C B A

Library of Congress Cataloging-in-Publication Data
Eklof, Barbara
Loving vows: inspiring promises for building and renewing your marriage / by Barbara Eklof.
p.   cm.
ISBN 1-58062-571-1
BL619.M37 E53   2001
392.5--dc21   2001046299

This publication is designed to provide accurate and authoritative information with regard to the subject matter covered. It is sold with the understanding that the publisher is not engaged in rendering legal, accounting, or other professional advice. If legal advice or other expert assistance is required, the services of a competent professional person should be sought.
—From a *Declaration of Principles* jointly adopted by a Committee of the American Bar Association and a Committee of Publishers and Associations

Cover photo by Rob Lewine/The Stock Market.

This book is available at quantity discounts for bulk purchases.
For information, call 1-800-872-5627.

Table of Contents

Introduction

The vision struck me like divine lightning. Couples need a book that answers the question, *Just as I expressed my marital promises through wedding vows, are there loving vows that can help show us how to keep these promises?*

Our wedding vows are essentially a recipe for a happy marriage. However, while consulting as the family relationship adviser for a popular Internet magazine, I became increasingly aware that most couples seldom turn to their wedding vows for guidance and perspective in times of need. This was evidenced by the advice thousands of husbands and wives sought. Their testimonies included *She promised to love me whether we were rich or poor, but . . .* or *We're fine during the "for better" times, but the moment things turn for the worse . . .* And far too many boiled down to *Love? After saying "I do," he forgot the meaning of the word.* It became clear to me that all too often our heartfelt wedding vows provide limited help with the actual marital experience.

I'm also the author of *With These Words...I Thee Wed: Wedding Vows for Today's Couples.* So, I certainly stand by the magnificent tradition of exchanging wedding vows. I feel that vows have the power to sustain us through every mile of this joyous, yet complex, relationship journey. But after the wedding ceremony dwindles into mounted snapshots, after the clinks of champagne toasts fade into memories, our sacred vows to one another too often collect dust in the corners of our minds. Couples are then left to manage marriage with the naive "good intentions" of a first date.

Unfortunately, civilization somehow forgot to develop a tradition that helps us keep our wedding vows alive. We have failed to build a bridge that links our wedding promises to marital realities. Thus, the vows we once held sacred are forgotten if "for better" fades into "for worse."

Realizing the difficulty so many couples have in fulfilling their vows, I thought: What if among the cherished clutter of wedding presents, newlyweds discovered a book that took their wedding vows to the next level? What if couples married over twenty years found a book that helped them enjoy their remaining years with fewer struggles? Wouldn't even unmarried lovers benefit from a book that laid out a step-by-step plan for a stronger relationship? *Yes,* I thought ecstatically, *indeed!*

Thus, *Loving Vows!* The book is divided into two parts. Part I provides marriage vows that originated from traditional wedding promises. Part II features marriage vows that originated from the most popular contemporary or personalized wedding pledges.

Each chapter features one heartfelt, helpful, and meaningful marriage vow per page. I encourage you and your spouse to exchange favorite vows during your honeymoon, during anniversary celebrations, and amid intimate discussions at home.

I hope these vows help you and your spouse to ignite newfound traditions and promote ongoing marital happiness. I hope you'll promise these vows to yourself, individually, in private determined moments. And I hope you'll turn to these vows for comfort and guidance in times of trouble.

Most of all, I wish everyone a happy and healthy marital journey.

Part I

From My Traditional Wedding Vows

Chapter 1

I Promised to Love

I promised to love you amid ceremony and witnesses. Now, I wish to ensure that my feelings are sustained and promoted for a lifetime.

Love

Love is so powerful that it's difficult to believe it's simply an emotion. Our love is as sacred as an altar where we light candles and fill our souls with peace. It is as beautiful as the view from the most majestic mountaintop, as exciting as a musical production that gains rave reviews. But alas, love is not a tangible object. It can't be touched or seen or heard in its truest sense. This is why I vow to show you my love as best I can, to radiate love so brightly from my eyes that you'll think they're sacred candles at an altar, to fill all I say and do with so much adoration that the view will leave you breathless, and to show so much affection and respect for you in public that if our love were a Broadway musical, it would get a standing ovation. ♥

Love and Marriage

The union between love and marriage is a charming exploration. For instance, and simply put, Have we ever considered that love was not made for marriage but that marriage was made for love? We can certainly love people, places, and things without the requirement of marriage. Yet love is the only proper prerequisite and guarantee to a happy marriage. Without love, what would a marriage be? This is why it's so important for us to protect our love and keep it safe and fresh. We must avoid any careless tendencies that could weaken our love, and we should forever monitor its strength, because love and marriage are both noble birthrights that should never be taken for granted. And so, my darling, for this perfect reason that we are married, I vow to find ways to love you well for all eternity. ❧

Unconditional Love

Spouses who are truly devoted to each other love unconditionally. They're nonjudgmental when listening to and advising their mate. As a result, their bonds deepen, and the love between them grows more magnificent in passing years. I want us to achieve this level of mutual devotion. So, I vow to practice unconditional love and a nonjudgmental attitude until both skills spring from my being naturally, without thought or plan. It'll simply be my way of loving you forever after. ❧

The Sentiment

If I can tailor my words to say "I love you" more magnificently, I will. If ever I envision a more creative means of showing my love, I'll do so. But for now, sweetheart, I vow to say "I love you" only when the meaning sings from my soul and dances through my limbs, when endless testimonies twirl through my thoughts and promises kept are gently recalled, when your aroma and touches sizzle my imagination, when missing you is anticipated or finally at an end, when your spirit heals my heart. In other words, when you hear me say "I love you," be assured that I mean it. ❧

Meaningful Kisses

Four lips meet at the stroke of desire, savoring the feeling, the closeness of love. Ah, the kiss. It's the blissful punctuation to any marital moment. Our kisses silently say *I forgive; I agree; thank you; I need you; I missed you.* They intimately seal our greetings and departures. Spousal kisses vow I love you and want you and only you forever and a day. Therefore, whether quick pecks or long passionate kisses, they allow us to send important messages. When most kisses become simply a reflex, without the slightest thought or meaning, we risk losing our mate's appreciation of these precious moments. With this in mind, I vow to fill each kiss with enough feeling to make an unforgettable statement.

Love and Laughter

When spouses are asked why they fell in love with their mates, it's amazing how many respond, "He/she made me laugh." And that reply always seems to accompany a special kind of smile, as if flashbacks of shared humor popped into the forefront of their minds. That's the magic of laughter between lovers. Humor is a buffer: The memories of fun times together linger in our souls and cushion us against bad memories long after the laughter ceases. Laughter is a referee: We sure can't stay angry after our mates crack a joke. And doing funny gestures keeps our spirits young. Do we feel young when tickling each other or making funny faces while in a tuxedo and gown? Of course! After all, the things that make us laugh together are just plain fun and refreshing? So with a joyful heart, I vow to turn up your smile and tickle your funny bone long into the golden years of our enjoyable romance. ❧

The Eyes of Love

The eyes of love see marvelous things. They see with protectiveness and adoration. We find ourselves fiercely defending our loved one against those who criticize unjustly. We find ourselves boasting to friends and family about the other's endearing ways and accomplishments. And when we're together, it's second nature for us to boost each other's confidence and esteem. It's nearly miraculous how some husbands see their wives as gorgeous when they're simply kind of cute and how some wives see kings before them when their husbands are truly shy. I'm so grateful to finally see through and be seen by the precious eyes of love that I vow to remain forever worthy of this rare vision from the heart. ❧

A Loving Nature

I pledge to develop my loving nature by keeping these guides in mind. Being LOVING means being:

Loyal—I offer my mate loving devotion so that we both may abide in the tranquility of trust.

Open—Being open and clear about my feelings is as much a show of love as being open to new ideas that inspire a lively marriage.

Valuable—I enjoy proving that my partner and our family are the most significant relationships in my life.

Imaginative—I find great pleasure in creating simple and lavish ways to say "I love you."

Negotiatory—Reaching compromises with my sweetheart confirms my desire to build our marriage as a loving team.

Gracious—I always show thankfulness for the multitude of joys that my partner and our wonderful marriage bring to my life. ౭

Chapter 2

I Promised to Cherish

Cherishing you forever was a promise I
happily made at our glorious wedding. Today,
I'll master the art of keeping this promise.

Cherishing Versus Loving

Yes dearest, I vowed to cherish you forever. At the time, though, the word *cherish* seemed synonymous with *love*. Now I realize the subtle distinction that makes all the difference. It's *because* I love you so divinely that I long to nurture your expectations, respect your sensibilities, and protect your peace. For this is how you cherish the one you hold dear. So, I pledge to remain mindful that by cherishing you, our cup will forever run over with love. 🖤

Appreciation

I vow to never stop appreciating you. This means that I will always be grateful for the value you bring to our marriage—everything you provide, everything you enhance, all that is better because of you. Too often couples dwell on the half-empty glass, seeing their spouse's flaws while overlooking the sacrifices that keep the glass half full. Not I. My outward show of thankfulness for all of your loving efforts will remain a treasure you can cherish forever. 🖤

Marital Friendship

It's great that we're not only lovers but that we're also best buddies. Friendship is the part of our relationship that inspires trust, loyalty, and also so much laughter. Being pals carries us into the light of each other's arms when the bliss dims. And by remembering to nurture this precious bond, we can rely upon its happy way of healing for all time. When all else fails, being each other's best friend must remain the glue of our unity. Therefore, I vow to nurture and enhance the qualities of our friendship as passionately as I do the qualities of our love. ❧

Cherishing

Why do I cherish you? You pledged your life to me. So, how could any other embrace compare to yours? How could any other eyes look upon me with the same adoration? You're intimately familiar with my strengths and weaknesses, yet you love me unconditionally. Our ultimate happiness depends upon our togetherness. You respect me, count on me, and love me sublimely. Truly, my love, I vow to honorably and adoringly and endlessly remember that you pledged your life to me! ❧

Cherishing or Smothering

How do people usually cherish treasured items? Some squeeze and hold them tight to their breast. Others find creative ways to keep their favorite memento forever by their side—at home, at work, even in the car. Although I feel extremely lucky to have you as my mate, although I cherish you far greater than any memento, I must not long to keep you forever by my side, in a literal sense. I must not desire to hold you forever to my breast. To do so is to smother the life out of our love. We both need personal space at times to explore individual emotions and thoughts and interests. Thus, because you're cherished so dearly, I vow to encourage and support your healthy personal space. ❧

Cherish

I pledge to show how much you are cherished in my life by following these helpful hints. I CHERISH you when I am being:

Comforting—No matter what difficulties you face in life, you'll always know that compassion is found at home.

Harmonious—No matter how trying your relationships may be with others, you can count on our spirit of togetherness.

Ernest—No matter how unsure you are of the responses of others, you'll always know that I speak the truth.

Reasonable—No matter how attentive you are to our marriage, you know I also understand your periodic need for space.

Innovative—No matter how routine life may seem at times, you know I always have a fun idea up my sleeve.

Sensual—No matter how stressed you may feel, you know I can soothe you with my alluring ways.

Happy—No matter how difficult it may seem to please others, you'll always know that simply the sight of you brightens my day.

Chapter 3

I Promised to Honor

Ever since our wedding day, honoring you as
my eternal beloved has been my utmost desire.
From this day forward, I yearn to do so more
effectively and with all my heart.

The Tradition of Marriage

I vow to bring honor to this glorious passage of our lives by staying mindful of why the tradition of marriage is so majestic:

- ❧ Marriage is the first and best of all human institutions.
- ❧ Marriage eternalizes the human race.
- ❧ Marriage lays the foundation for organized societies worldwide.
- ❧ Marriage promotes industry and economics.
- ❧ Marriage cultivates the arts and maintains religious and spiritual beliefs.
- ❧ Marriage supports the family and fosters every charitable and benevolent cause.

Every person of each gender—whether rich or poor, in sickness or health—is entitled to the rights and benefits of this perfect and loving time-honored tradition. ❧

Special Occasions

I pledge to honor you and our union by remembering our special occasions and by making them meaningful. Your birthday holds special significance because you were born to be my beloved. Our wedding anniversaries commemorate the years our souls have danced as one. Mother's Day and Father's Day celebrate the family our union created. And holidays ignite ancient traditions that gleefully bond families for all times. Between these splendid occasions of honor, I'll gladly join in celebrating everything, from your promotions to athletic victories to everyday joys. Because honoring you is not only a joy to me, it helps create beautiful tomorrows. ❧

The Gift of Giving

I vow to honor you with spirit-lifting gifts throughout the years—not only during momentous holidays and anniversaries and birthdays but also for no particular occasion. It's the little everyday efforts from the heart that are often the most appreciated. A simple grocery errand becomes a romantic occasion when I return with the gift of a single rose. The surprise of cologne found tucked in a briefcase inspires the sweetest thoughts. Regardless of the occasion, gifts made by hand become cherished keepsakes. That's why gifts such as a favorite homemade cake inspire special moments and memories. It's so meaningful when I also make a point to remember an item or an experience that you've longed for and then surprise you with it. I feel this way because fostering your ongoing happiness is my greatest gift of all. ✿

Give-and-Take

Understanding how to honor you while mastering the art of give-and-take isn't always easy. I want to maintain my individuality and, at the same time, be able to compromise with you. Both are vital for marital bliss. So, I vow to be patient and accept you for who you are; focusing on your positive traits elevates your self-confidence and our marital happiness. Rather than trying to change you, we'll discuss how we'll both change over the years. Instead of measuring who's offering our marriage the most, I'll adopt a team spirit, realizing that we each pull our own weight as needed and at different times. And although I won't hesitate to be good to myself, I won't become so self-absorbed that I lose sight of being good to us. ❧

Representing Us

Through the divine passage of marriage, we are no longer two separate individuals who are accountable for ourselves alone. We're soul mates who found and recognized each other, then fell completely in love. We became each other's sweetest half of a remarkable couple. And now we're partners in the ultimate venture of marriage. Because of our history, past and future, my words and actions are no longer reflections of me alone. Everything I do and say mirrors you as well. So, when I'm working and playing and socializing, although onlookers are observing *my* behavior, they're usually assessing us both. *That's so-and-so's wife/husband,* they might think. And I want us both to be proud of that assessment. Therefore, my dearest, this is my vow: I will forever honor you and our marriage by representing us both in a manner that lives up to my personal best and your most comforting expectations.

Honor

I vow to forever honor you and our sublime marriage by practicing these relationship pointers. I show my dearest HONOR when I am:

Helpful—Offering a helpful hand, an encouraging word, and a useful idea are just some of the ways I show the value of you in my life.

Overjoyed—Sharing in your enthusiasm and excitement enhances your special moments and shows that I'm truly proud of all of your goals and accomplishments, no matter how great or small.

Nice—A spirit of kindness, thoughtfulness, and generosity—expressed simply or ceremonially—shows my admiration for our relationship as lifetime friends and lovers.

Oblivious—Ignoring your imperfections while celebrating your wonderful attributes strengthens your self-esteem and affirms how much I adore you, just the way you are.

Respectable—Whether together or apart, I conduct myself in public in a manner that makes you proud, that reflects kindly on our marriage, and that honors my happiness as your mate. ❧

Chapter 4

I Promised to Obey

Promising to obey often causes us a bit of confusion, since it seems to imply inequality in the relationship. However, it doesn't have to. Because I did vow to obey, it's important that I understand how to apply this pledge to my fulfilling life as your partner.

Obey My Vows

With the greatest sincerity, I vow to obey every marital promise I made to you at the altar before family and witnesses. May you never think of me as deceitful or untrustworthy, as careless or indifferent with my words. When we're in our twilight years, I hope you consider our long marriage the most special relationship of your existence. I want you to know and remember me as loving and honoring, forsaking all others through sickness and health, for richer or poorer. My vows to you, darling, were more than promises. My vows were guiding lights that I will forever follow. ❧

Obey My Conscience

Although we all have imperfections, I know right from wrong. I value integrity and strive to achieve exemplary ideals. Being a good person and mate is important to me. Being accountable for my decisions is more of a lifestyle than a task. Our conscience is an inner voice that protects and warns us from anything we might do that can harm us. Therefore, I vow to listen to and obey my conscience at all times, especially when tempted to do anything that could damage you, our marriage, our family, or myself. &

Obey My Logic

It's important that we allow our reasoning abilities to override poor actions and decisions that are based purely on emotions. Doing so inspires us to compromise on decisions and plans, for instance, because we are a team of two loving adults. Our rational minds enable us to see and address larger concerns when we're tempted to quibble over unrelated trivial matters, such as complaining about poor table manners when we're really upset about the mishandled budget. And shouldn't we take time to calmly question and analyze annoying situations, such as one of us arriving home later than expected, before making accusations or showing our annoyance? Mostly, when we assess all the situations that led to our amazing marriage and all that we've overcome and built together since, it's our logical minds that remind us just how precious our union truly is. So, I vow to remember that the beauty of following my logic is that it keeps situations in perspective and me balanced. ♥

Obey My Spirit of Equality

Throughout our marital journey, there will be times when we'll take turns being fairer and more insightful than the other. This is good, because a marriage is as strong as the values, knowledge, life experiences, and reasoning abilities that both mates bring to it. Even if one mate led a sheltered life, he or she must be given opportunities to make decisions and share ideas that are respected. And if these decisions or notions reach a disappointing end, the only feedback that partner should hear is understanding and encouragement to try again. This is how we, as individuals, spread our wings and grow. This is how we, as eternal mates, learn mutual respect and bond even closer. Husbands and wives are both flourishing individuals with experiences and dreams of their own. Marriage is the bridge that united these experiences and dreams into a flowing life of love. And the spirit of equality pays honor and tribute to the only person in the world who vowed to help keep my future experiences and dreams lovely and alive. Indeed, I pledge to embrace my spirit of equality for as long as I wear the title "Your Life Partner," which will be forever and a day. ✍

Obey My Dreams

Some spouses only *talk* about their ambitions; some *do* what it takes to make them a reality. We all have personal and marital dreams for the future. The thought of reaching them inspires us to get out of bed in the morning, surmount obstacles, take risks, stay our personal best, and learn whatever's needed. Life feels so worthwhile. In other words, we run a good race to the GOAL line. Yet because some of us allow daily routines and pressures to slow us down, that goal line can start to appear unreachable. Some mates or couples even give up and coast for the rest of their unfulfilled lives. But if we took at least thirty minutes out of each day to accomplish something toward an important goal—to plant a seed no matter how great or small—we'd be amazed how our dreams take root and grow. If needed, I'll awake thirty minutes earlier or retire to bed later, use half of my lunch hour, or start a carpool for the children and make good use of those driving-free days. Indeed, I vow to know the bliss of realizing my dreams by obeying the maxim: Where there's a will, there's a way! &

Obey My Spiritual Beliefs

I do not embrace and exhibit my spiritual beliefs for show or image. Rather, I strive to be at peace with everyone and everything and every place I encounter. When I embrace peace, I feel more in harmony with the universe, and that feeling enables me to exhibit greater understanding and patience with our family. I can enhance our marriage with greater contentment and loving expectations. Life feels good. And so, I vow to strengthen and obey my spiritual nature while allowing it to guide me through this beautiful creation called "us." ❧

Obey My Heart

I understand the cliché Love conquers all. After a heated squabble, suppose I wrote a list of reasons I should and reasons I should not forgive my partner. Although my "should not" list might be a mile long, my "should" list would win with this single note: *Because I love her/him.* And I would indeed forgive my beloved. That's why I'm fascinated by the power love has over opposing emotions of the heart, emotions such as sadness, hurt, and anger. Because no matter how dispirited we may feel at times, a simple kiss, a tender embrace, and an understanding word can not only reunite our hearts with gladness but also hold the key to filling our hearts with forgiveness. And for all the times we're tempted by wrongdoing or we simply need a bit of marital motivation, we can turn to our hearts—which store the feelings behind our every kiss, embrace, and loving memory—and stay strong and delightfully focused. After all, our marriage and family mean everything to us. For these reasons and many more, I vow to you, my darling, that when all else fails in putting me back on a healthy marital track, I will listen to my heart and rise into your arms.

Obey

I pledge to keep the word OBEY in perspective by staying mindful of these marital ideals:

Objectivity—Instead of concentrating on who made the best decision, partners with healthy and fair marriages obey their logic and focus on what the best decisions are for their future happiness.

Boldness—It may take courage and willpower to maintain obedience to our values and beliefs, yet the prize of a peaceful happy family is well worth the effort.

Efficiency—Obeying an ethical mindset creates a sense of order that both simplifies and embellishes our daily lives as loving partners.

Yes, commitment—We now are of one yoke and yearn for a lifetime of bliss. So, to all the healthy values, beliefs, and teachings that ensure our longevity, we answer the calls to obey with a resounding "Yes, I will!" ♔

Chapter 5

I Promised Faithfulness

I promised to forsake all others at our wedding
because I love you above all others and chose
to be with you and only you. Now, let's be
sure to keep that promise alive.

Avoiding Infidelities

It's vital that I maintain respect for my partner and my marriage. Although we are living in times when even public role models are setting poor fidelity examples, I will rise above their careless actions and keep my mind and body pure for my mate. This is a gift that only I can decide upon. Faithfulness is a goal that proves my character. In light of this, I vow to never entertain adulterous thoughts nor acknowledge any behaviors from others that might tempt any form of infidelity. ❧

Temptation

Ah, forbidden fruit: It's amazing how what we don't and can't have can appear so appealing. And yet, from money to chocolate, temptations can be our doom. Bank robbers are imprisoned, overeaters may decline in health, and spouses who embrace extramarital affairs often end up divorced! So, if tempted by an affair, I vow to ask myself these questions and take action:

Question: What do I see in this person that I don't see in my mate?
Action: Discuss with my mate to see if these needs can be met.

Question: Is physical attraction my only temptation?
Action: Envision my tempter far older, unattractive, and with disgusting habits.

Question: Why did I fall in love with my mate?
Action: Make a list and refer to it for control when needed. ✑

Needing a Challenge

I vow to keep my need for challenges in perspective. Needing challenges is a trait that's inherent in us all. This is why sports and games are so popular and why gaining well-deserved job promotions is so rewarding. There's nothing like the luscious taste of victory. But when it comes to needing challenges in our relationships, sometimes the sport is sweeter than the victory. In other words, if a spouse has not directed his or her conquering spirit in healthier directions, the victory of winning such a wonderful mate may soon dwindle into feelings of boredom—that the challenge is over and your mate is now a sure thing. This misguided pursuit of challenges can lead to extramarital affairs. What a never-ending cycle of discontent for anyone to bear. Contentment lies in gaining a spouse who makes all of my dreams come true and then creating new dreams together. The excitement stems from buying our first home together, or having a baby, or planning a second honeymoon, or watching our kids succeed, or celebrating our golden wedding anniversary, or knowing you chose me for life. The list is endless, because the greatest challenge that I now face is keeping our marriage happy, healthy, and alive with love. ❧

Vanity and Low Self-Esteem

If a spouse has a low self-esteem, the love of one mate may not seem enough. He or she may "need" additional attention and admiration of and seduction from people outside of the marriage, in order to feel valued and complete. And this attitude and behavior can lead to an adulterous affair. It's important that each mate develop a strong sense of self-worth and wholeness in order to realize the faithfulness to one partner that a marriage requires. Therefore, if I have issues due to a low self-esteem and I'm not offering my mate the respect and loyalty he or she deserves, I vow to seek counseling and discuss these challenges with my mate until we both are assured of a devoted relationship. 🙏

No Meeting,
No Cheating

I vow to join the ranks of the wise mates, who prevent sticky situations with the opposite sex by avoiding hazardous conditions,
such as frequenting nightclubs alone. Careful mates know that
because alcohol lowers inhibitions and good judgment, vulnera-
bility increases. And they seldom party without their partners
joining them in the fun. If a coworker or social club member
sends flirtatious signals, cautious spouses defuse the slightest
possibility of an affair. They do this by evading, say, one-on-one
lunches with those who have more than friendship in mind.
They only talk to these people in positive terms about their
spouses, and they show flattering fun pictures of their mates and
families. Above all, they never discuss their marital sex lives. I'm
proud to be among the wise, careful, and cautious mates who
know how to say, "No!" ℘

Truth and Explanations

As loving partners, we deserve the truth from each other. If one of us makes a questionable statement, the other has the right to ask for and receive clarity. If either of our routines and habits change abruptly without a reasonable cause, the mate who questions this is due a straightforward and logical explanation. As spouses, it's our responsibility to make certain the other understands the reasons for our behavior, doing so provides peace of mind and soothes the hearts of us both. For indeed, successfully comforting my beloved feels just as rewarding as being comforted. Therefore, we vow to talk out all concerns until both parties are peacefully assured and to seek professional guidance if needed. ❧

Ending an Infidelity

If I have not lived up to my wedding vows, while showing signs of immaturity and insensitivity, I pledge to correct my conduct immediately. If I have been disloyal, I vow to put a stop to this troubling behavior and never turn back. If I've been deceptive, I pledge to revert to honesty until my every action is pleasing to my mate. If I've lacked respect for my partner's feelings, I vow to soar to higher levels of sensitivity and empathy, while making it my undying duty to reset this marriage on solid ground. 🙟

Confessing an Infidelity

I realize that confessing unfaithful behavior is not only beneficial to my own peace of mind but also crucial to the soundness of this marriage. Though I may fear risking a loss of trust and even a breakup, I'll also be proving that I'm strong enough and reliable enough to take responsibility for my own actions. And I hope—despite the pain I've caused, despite the admission that I've defiled our sacred wedding vows—my beloved will find faith in my desire to heal and reconcile our union, which I do indeed hold dear. So, instead of carrying the burden of these shameful secrets another second, I vow to bring rest to my partner's suspicions by rising immediately to his/her expectations of truthfulness. ৯৯

Asking Forgiveness

If I am worthy of forgiveness, then I can ask for it. Neither my ego nor pride should stand in the way. During my wedding vows, I promised before my spouse and witnesses to be faithful. And yet, I let them all down. I let myself down. And I've not known a moment of peaceful happiness since. This is because my body and mind and spirit cannot serve two mates. I brought my beloved to the altar of marriage with the best of intentions. Now, to rededicate myself to this marriage, I vow to seek and become worthy of my beloved's forgiveness. ❧

Forgiving an Infidelity

When I entered this marriage, I knew a day might come that would test my pledge to remain married even during the worst of times. That day has come. My mate has betrayed my trust and our marriage. My pain is deep and real and makes me want to run far away. And yet, how can I fault my mate for breaking his/her sacred wedding vow to remain faithful if I also break my vow to remain in this marriage for better or worse? And any thoughts of revenge would only worsen matters, while adding to the negative energy. Forgiving a wrong is often difficult, but it is extremely necessary for the salvation of our union and my own peace of mind. I must remember my mate's strong qualities and weigh them against this one great mistake, because I'd want forgiveness if I ever erred for any reason. And running away at the first sign of real trouble is the reason the divorce rate is so high. I, for one, did not enter this marriage to become a statistic. I entered for keeps! Therefore, I pledge to forgive my mate while learning all I can about recovering from an infidelity and while reaching out for all the support I need. ✐

Healing from an Infidelity

Although it's difficult to believe, recovering from an infidelity has its bright side. Once my mate has taken responsibility for his or her actions by giving a full accounting, we can open doors to having positive discussions about our relationship and where it has declined. We'll decide how to carefully put our marriage back in order, which I understand won't happen overnight. It's my mate's responsibility to constantly reassure me in every way imaginable that the affair is truly over and will never happen again. And since our sexual attraction for each other is usually the last thing that's restored, we'll rely upon nonsexual touching, intimate chats, and anything that aides in rebuilding trust in the meantime. My spouse and I now vow together to abide by these and all guidelines that heal a weakened marriage, until we've built a stronger union. ❧

Trust

We vow to help maintain TRUST between us by following these guidelines:

Truth—We'll keep our integrity at all times by providing accurate information.

Respect—All of our actions and words will honor the sanctity of our marriage.

Understanding—We'll relieve all doubts and concerns the other may have.

Spirituality—We'll strive to follow our spiritual beliefs and consciences.

Tenacity—Maintaining trust will be our never-ending goal. ❦

Chapter 6

I Promised: For Better or for Worse

Promising to sustain our marriage through the good times and the bad times is often easier to vow than to achieve. In order to make sure we're ready for the good times and the bad, let's anticipate problems, be adaptable to change, and make preventative plans whenever we can.

Optimistic or Pessimistic

I vow to think "success" amid all of our endeavors. Too many spouses forget that thoughts have energy. I can make my world or break it by my thoughts alone. If I anticipate disappointment or defeat, I'm gravitating toward and even causing a negative end. But when I remain optimistic and anticipate triumphant outcomes, my positive energy lures satisfying results. In other words, my efforts are guided by my attitude, and my attitude is guided by my thoughts. I want us to be a productive couple, content in the knowledge that the only limits we possess are those we place upon ourselves. ✌

Lovemaking or Sex

I will remember the vast difference between making love and
simply engaging in sexual activities. Making love is the mutual
desire to share a level of intimacy that transcends having sex,
which is simply bodily gratification. Indeed, making love is
sometimes even void of sexual contact. The warm exchanges we
share—such as simply holding each other, or those lingering
kisses when departing and returning from work, or even helping
the other find or fix an item of sentimental value—inspire our
mutual affection. And affection should be the precursor and
aftermath to a wondrous lovemaking encounter. Absolutely, I
vow to make all of our moments of intimacy a memorable and
meaningful experience for us both. ๛

Well Groomed or Unkempt

The familiarity of our spouses sometimes causes us to relax our attitudes and even our grooming practices, when in actuality the opposite should prevail. Simply because I gained my dream mate, I shouldn't let my original alluring traits slip into oblivion. I should demonstrate the respect I have for both of us by staying healthy and fit, updating my wardrobe periodically, and keeping my hair neat and stylish. And simply because I may have a favorite outfit for leisurely home time, I shouldn't wear it daily like a uniform—rips, stains, and all. Because I wish to remain enticing to my mate, I vow to maintain good grooming and personal hygiene habits, even when casually relaxing. &

Gracious or Taken for Granted

How sad it is when mates began to take each other's efforts for granted. The meals that were once praised, the repairs that were so appreciated, gradually slip into the ungracious abyss of expected duties. And the sweet compliments that once lifted our spirits are replaced with a sense of emptiness, even servitude. Positive reinforcement is needed at home as much as it is in the workplace. Recognition of our spouse's efforts, great and small, not only validates his or her value as a mate but also encourages more of what we appreciate about the other. I pledge to maintain a gracious spirit and to never take my beloved for granted.

A Marriage
or a Game

Too many mates enter matrimony as if it were a game: If we win, we stay together; if we lose, we sadly but simply divorce. Marriage is not a game. In fact, if we avoided many of the characteristics games possess, we could strengthen our beautiful union. For instance, games inspire risk taking that can result in devastation, if my choices or luck should reach an undesired end. Unlike in a Monopoly game, in which losing money and going to jail are part of the fun, mates should avoid risks that could put the entire marriage in serious jeopardy. When we play most board games, the money is fake, the stakes are unreal, and the dramatic outcome, whether we win or lose, is fleeting. So, I vow to remember that marriage is not a game of luck, in which we gamble on the outcome of "us." Our sacred union, though fun, is real and serious, and I will ensure that it lasts for the rest our lives. &

A Team or Competitors

Healthy competition is encouraged in sports and even in many work situations. But rivalry between spouses is taboo. It's unproductive and jeopardizes our marital stability. Vying over, say, who makes the most money or who's the most romantic or who's the smartest creates strife, division. We're unique individuals with different strengths and weaknesses. Together we're an awesome team. That's why we must vow to alert the other when comparisons enter our conversations. Instead, we'll keep our competitive spirits in their proper arenas, while filling our home with the bliss of unity. ❧

Spontaneity or Ruts

Our marital journey can take many unexpected bends. It's particularly easy to slide into the doldrums of daily routine. It's our marital duty to keep the relationship fresh with spontaneity, surprises, and eroticism. I can transform Wednesday's fish stick dinner into a romantic candlelit fare of finger food and wine. I might surprise you and offer myself for lunch on a workday, at a convenient motel. We should take periodic exotic trips, with weekend escapes in between, play "footsies" under the breakfast table, and send romantic e-mail to each other (be careful doing that at the office, though!). We should prepare scented bubble baths for two and slow dance on our starlit patio. With so many options available, I vow to help keep our marriage alive with spontaneity and imagination. ✎

Partners or Entertainers

I shouldn't feel the pressure of having to keep you entertained at all times. That's quite a chore to maintain for a lifetime. As a healthy couple, we should be able to share the same space while each is doing his or her own thing. There's no need to chat when there's nothing in particular to say. It's okay to be alone with our private thoughts. Although it's important to keep our relationship lively, it's just as important to relax in our leisure time without feeling bored. Truly, I vow to remember that the sign of a healthy couple is one who is content doing nothing, either together or apart. Just knowing you're comfortably in my life is enough. ❧

In Sync or Offbeat

The unfortunate excuse too many couples offer for a failed marriage is "We outgrew each other." To avoid this or any other excuse for a breakup, it's important that we hear the same beat. We can do this by communicating regularly about our goals, expectations, and concerns. We should ensure that our lifestyle, social experiences, and friends are still pleasing to both. We should be prepared to compromise and make fair changes to avoid incompatibility. That's why I vow to keep you abreast of my desires and misgivings and to always make yours my top priority. I'll do this with an ultimate goal in mind: growing together. ✍

Rebounding or
Passive

I pledge to remember that it doesn't matter how often we slip into valleys but rather how quickly we rise from them. Since hardships are inevitable, we must keep them in perspective. Instead of dwelling on our misfortunes, which will keep us stagnant, we'll celebrate each small step toward progress. Maintaining an optimistic view of our situation makes all the difference between rebounding quickly or lingering passively in negativity and doubt. I want to spend most of our marriage enjoying the love we share, so I now claim an optimistic attitude during both struggles and times of peace. ❧

Friends or Troublemakers

I vow to remain discerning about the people shared in our lives. Sadly, for whatever reason, not everyone's intentions are honorable. If we encounter friends or family members who disrespectfully intrude upon our union, we will not allow them to disrupt our happiness. For the sake of our longevity, our circle of support must consist of loved ones who truly respect us as a couple and care about our well-being. And with the same care in which we chose each other, we will be equally wise when choosing our marital advisers and confidants and close friends. 🙞

Happiness at Home
or Elsewhere

Sometimes during the course of a marriage, a partner begins to seek his or her ultimate satisfaction from external sources. Greater amounts of energy then go toward, say, developing career goals rather than maintaining a happy home. Or joining numerous organizations or socializing with buddies may intrude on the quality time normally spent with our mates. We all yearn to be appreciated and to make our marks in life. But it's a mistake to do so at the expense of our marital homes. When external regrets and disappointments arrive, for instance, it's home where we seek refuge and comfort. For this reason and many others, I vow that I will never jeopardize or minimize the value of my marital home, or take it for granted. Yes, I will develop a full satisfying life, but I'll do so in sync with my marital priorities. ❦

Capable or Inadequate

I understand that marriage is never truly 50/50. Sometimes one partner will carry a heavier load than the other, and then the situation will reverse. That's the inevitable seesaw syndrome. One spouse may be jobless when the other isn't. Or one may keep the peace when the other's being moody. Peaks and valleys are the norms of life, and personal downtime in no way reflects our ultimate capabilities. This is why I vow that I will never make you feel inadequate during difficult situations, or belittle you by displaying a superior attitude. Instead, I'll enjoy remaining your greatest source of kindness and inspiration and have faith that we'll both ultimately land on our feet. ❧

Partner or Controller

We are two whole individuals who are now joined as one. We each have the right to enjoy our friends and family, careers and hobbies, and personal interests. We're both adults. As partners in love and life, we must respect each other as equals. Our relationship should be void of tests, character assassinations, superior attitudes, and dictatorship. Our home must remain warm and welcoming and never feel like a prison. In other words, neither of us has the right to control the other emotionally, spiritually, or physically. I vow that I'll never seek control over my mate or accept controlling situations. If I experience such behavior, I also vow to seek marriage counseling immediately. ❧

Content or Envious

Marriage envy—it's those hidden glances toward a couple, maybe while socializing, who seem to be fulfilling a marital fantasy we've yet to obtain. Maybe they're being more affectionate or playful, or perhaps they seem more secure. Actually, I shouldn't feel guilty for watching another couple enviously, nor should I be upset if I catch my mate doing the same. Instead, we should discuss what we like about the other couple's actions, which in turn will allow us to monitor our marital satisfaction and fantasies. Then we can adopt these enviable traits and make them our own. After all, the sky is the limit when it comes to creating a happier marriage for us both. Therefore, I vow to keep our marriage content by switching from being envious of another couple to learning new practices that will keep our own union fresh and alive. ❧

Secure or Jealous

Of all the mates you could have chosen, you chose me. I vow to remain secure in that knowledge and to raise my esteem above petty jealousies. I admire couples who can go to social gatherings and feel perfectly comfortable splitting up and hobnobbing with separate friends. That's such a show of trust. Yet their ultimate joy is apparent when they finally reunite. Neither slips into the clinging vine syndrome, trying to show ownership by hanging on to his or her partner's arm. Insecure mates even watch to see whom of the opposite sex their partner talks to or laughs with the longest. This isn't characteristic of a secure, happy relationship. By trusting and offering space, I'm showing that I have confidence in us both. ❦

Compromise or Stubbornness

I promise to remember that compromise is the key to developing marital peace. The way I handled situations and made decisions when I was single must be reconsidered. I am now half of a glorious united couple. Together we can find ways to work as a team for the sake of our long-term happiness. Therefore, with all the love in which I entered this marriage, I vow to make certain that all actions and decisions are of one accord with my loving mate. ❧

Love or Abuse

Abusive marriages are not made in heaven and shouldn't endure. Amid any marital crisis, marriage or family counseling is advisable. However, if any form of mental, physical, or sexual abuse is present, an immediate safe separation is prudent. In other words, in this case, "for better or worse" does not apply! Love and marriage is not synonymous with hurt, pain, and fear. Therefore, if my marriage is damaged by abusive behavior, I vow to hope beyond hope, relocate to a safe haven, and heal. ❧

Challenges or Problems

I vow to keep problems in perspective by reassessing them in a more positive light. PROBLEMS are:

Predictors—They warn us about disasters.

Reminders—We're not always self-sufficient. We need faith, family, and friends to help.

Opportunities—They pull us from our ruts and cause us to think creatively.

Blessings—They open doors that we seldom enter.

Lessons—Each new challenge becomes a teacher.

Educational—They prove just how resourceful and tenacious we are.

Measurable—We can prioritize them and not let them grow out of proportion.

Solvable—No problem is without a solution! ✍

Chapter 7

I Promised: For Richer or for Poorer

I vowed to commit to you for richer or for poorer.
Now, to strengthen this pledge, my greatest desire
is to master the art of being content regardless of
our financial situation.

Employment

Employment choices vary from family to family. For many couples, having a stable and secure home life necessitates two incomes, one from each spouse. Some spouses decide to live on one income so that their mates may care for the children and/or the household with consistency. And some mates take on more than one job while their spouses pursue educational or entrepreneurial goals. Today, spouses have a wealth of choices that are free of gender bias and stereotypes. Based on desire or priorities or whose income is the most adequate, it's not uncommon to find stay-at-home husbands and dads. And many spouses opt to work from home, which affords a lovely blend of career satisfaction and family care. Understanding these choices, I vow to remain open-minded as my beloved and I design an employment lifestyle that benefits each family member and our future goals. &

Unemployment

Because the business world is often unpredictable, my mate or I may experience temporary unemployment. If this happens to my partner, I vow to remember that my beloved needs time to grieve over this career loss. I'll offer encouragement instead of criticism, and a helping hand—such as sprucing up a resume or taking his or her interview suit to the cleaners—instead of resentment. I'll support my mate if he or she chooses a lesser job until the dream job comes along; after all, he or she has chosen family survival over selfish pride. And if that dream job becomes too elusive and we can no longer run a comfortable household, I vow to remain understanding and flexible as my beloved learns a new skill, obtains a degree, or re-enters the job market. In other words, I will treat my mate exactly as I would like to be treated if the situation were reversed.

Home Management

The "business of life" must be handled with the same diligence and planning as any profession. Life's business consists of the day-to-day responsibilities we undertake to ensure a well-managed home and relationship. For instance, paying bills on time—it's a chore only if we're disorganized. By establishing one or two dates per month for paying bills, we avoid the hassles, penalties, and inconvenience. We must also remain attentive to banking matters, income taxes, vehicle and home and lawn upkeep, shopping for essentials, and so on. Developing a budget and sticking to it is wise, and carefully filing important documents such as warrantees and guarantees is vital. To ensure a smooth running home and marriage, I vow to become an organized home management pro. ❦

The Nature of Free Happiness

I'm constantly amazed by the year-round joys life offers so freely. Come summer, I love our reflections in the water while strolling by ponds, and the tickle of lush grass beneath our bare feet. Romancing under fall stars to the tune of rustling jewel-colored leaves makes my imagination soar. The elation of winter snowball fights can only compare to the soothing grace of sharing hot cider before a flickering fire. And the birth of spring inspires those long lazy drives through landscapes blooming with pastels. Let's vow to always value and share Earth's abundance year-round, no matter our incomes, no matter our lifestyle. 🖋

Rich or Successful

I pledge to remain modest if my mate and I reach higher levels of financial security or personal success. Although increased finances afford us the opportunity to improve our living condition and lifestyle, and although reaching a personal goal may boost our self-esteem, money or success should never change our personalities, unless it's for the better. If we have been concerned about the plight of the less fortunate or about the environment, now we may have more time for proactive gestures. If a friend or family member incurs a financial crisis, now we can offer financial assistance or share how we obtained our good fortune. All the while, we will temper these acts of kindness and generosity with humility, because the way we appear to those in the world around us is a reflection upon our character as a married couple. ❧

Fantasies of Wealth

Some spouses dream of trading their routine lives for those of wealthier couples who appear so exciting and carefree. They must think, *If only we could travel on a whim like so-and-so,* or *If only we could have servants at our beck and call.* It's perfectly normal to fantasize about the lifestyles of the rich and famous; these types of day-dreams motivate us to improve our circumstances. The trick is to keep such thoughts in perspective. Too often couples waste away the here and now by dwelling on the what if. What good is it to finally reach financial wealth if, in the process, your neglected relationship has become weak? Did you make your partner feel that your marriage, before the wealth arrived, was not good enough and that you were not content? If so, would he or she remain interested in sharing the trips and servants with you? Whether such dreams are obtained, we must always take time to notice and develop the wonderful marriage we have today. With this in mind, I vow contentment, while making certain that our present lifestyle is worth its weight in gold. ❧

A Rich Marriage

I vow to remember that the richness of a marriage is not measured by financial wealth. A rich MARRIAGE is:

Motivating—We inspire the other person's mental, physical, and financial well-being.

Abundant—We ensure ongoing fun, peace, and mutual fascination.

Resilient—We work together to rise above all difficulties.

Rational—We avoid unrealistic expectations and unreasonable demands.

Intimate—We cherish the private side of our love and life.

Absolute—We retain unlimited thinking, pure behavior, and unconditional love.

Generous—We flourish emotional and affordable shows of appreciation on each other.

Equal—We treat each other as responsible adults.

Chapter 8

I Promised: In Sickness and in Health

When we met at the altar of matrimony, we vowed
to care for each other in sickness and in health.
I want to be prepared and there for you through all
possibilities, just as you would be for me.

Dependability

Our union must far outweigh the superficial. We must be ready for life's changes and challenges and strong enough to be there for each other even when times are tough. So, by promising to stay whole through sickness and health, we're attesting to a relationship of substance, reliability, and accountability, to a union in which we're there for each other through the bright and dark seasons of life. Therefore, because my love knows no boundaries, I pledge to remain just as dependable through the storms of illness as I would want you to be for me. ❧

Medical Care

There are many ways to help my partner when he or she is ill. Doctors specializing in a wide array of medical practices now have Web pages brimming with advice. We can easily visit the Internet, instead of the local drugstore, to check whether a prescription is refillable. We can even have lab reports sent to our e-mail addresses. So, gladly I vow to be the best partner I can be when an illness strikes our union, by doing everything possible to nurse you back to health, from taking your temperature, to researching remedies on the Web, to just holding your hand for comfort. ❧

Menopause

Contrary to popular beliefs, our postmenopausal years—generally after age fifty—promise greater contentment and sexual pleasures than our earlier years of marriage. Back then, raising a family and riding employment fast tracks distracted us from completely relaxing together, but now we can. Sure, our emotions may seem a bit topsy-turvy at times, and patience may wear thin. But this too shall pass. And with the children grown and on their own, we'll feel like newlyweds again, free to explore life and love with newfound appreciation. What a pleasure to pledge continued patience and understanding during the menopausal transition. We've had a wonderful lifetime of practicing for and perfecting the second chapter of our lives. ❧

Healthy Aging

So many spouses are living to be 100 and older because we understand that aging well means living well. And the keys to longevity are our mental and emotional attitudes. Yes, we diet and exercise and realize that it's never too late to start a healthier regime. But equally vital is that we exercise our minds. For instance, we replace passive TV watching with mental stimuli like working puzzles, surfing the Internet, and reading. Surely, we vow to add quality to our golden years with each other by establishing or continuing healthy aging practices. ❧

Fountain of Youth

With the kids grown and gone, life's luster may dim into a blur of routine. Even the love songs that once sparked romance are barely noticed over sighed duets of "Oh, to be young again." But we can be! Now there's more time to recapture the whimsical little things that made life fun and exciting, that made us feel young and frivolous! So we vow to kick out those rocking chairs and follow some of these paths to the fountain of youth:

- Run in the rain.
- Dance on a beach.
- Rent sexy movies.
- Throw parties.
- Visit carnivals.
- Share sundaes.
- Fulfill dreams.
- Climb a tree.
- Fly a kite.
- Blow bubbles.
- Play games.
- Giggle a lot.
- Whistle.
- Hug a lot.

Eldercare

Planning early for our eldercare can help to relieve my spouse of trying decisions and possible feelings of guilt. If I'm unable to care for myself, who will care for me, and where? Are there friends or family members willing and able to help my mate with this responsibility? Would I prefer home care by a visiting nurse? Or am I comfortable moving to an assisted-living residence for seniors or to a nursing home for total care? Finally, if I should reach a state of unrecoverable unconsciousness and my beloved must decide my life-support fate, what is my wish? I vow to discuss these matters with my partner with honesty, understanding, and tenderness. ✍

Empathy

Above all, I vow to offer the same EMPATHY and loving care to you in sickness as in health. So, my darling, should you become ill in any manner, you'll find me to be:

Enjoyable—I'll lift our spirits with laughter and motivate us through music. I'll refresh us with cool breezes and warm sunshine. And I'll take us on adventures by reading books by your side.

Merciful—I'll care for your needs with the same patience and loving kindness as you would offer so liberally to me.

Protective—I'll ensure that you have the best medical attention, visitors full of goodwill, and prayers for a speedy recovery.

Affirming—You'll always know that my efforts come naturally from a loving heart.

Tactful—You'll hear only patient words of encouragement, empathy, and love.

Hopeful—I'll see that we both remain pleasantly optimistic at all times.

Yours—For better or worse, I'll be there for you with a benevolent spirit. ❧

Chapter 9

I Promised: Till Death Do Us Part

I pledged to love you and remain the best mate possible until death do us part. And although thinking of our inevitable life separation through death is difficult, in my heart I know I must prepare for this eventual passage of our lives.

Making Peace with Death

Births, weddings, anniversaries—we generally understand these major passages of life and anticipate them with much fore-thought. Yet it's often difficult to give the same consideration to our own or our spouse's passage into death. Still, when we don't take time to process the stages of dying and bereavement, we're often left to juggle emotions that range from grief to guilt to utter confusion. Therefore, we vow to lighten each other's poten-tial distress by discussing our physical transitions from life in an open and sincere manner. Talks will include topics such as per-sonalized funeral plans to ensure our wishes are achieved, how my survivor can find peace in due time and carry on with a healthy productive life, and how we'll love through death as we loved through life. ❧

Letter of Resolution

I pledge to write a personal letter of resolution to my spouse, to be sealed and stored with other important documents and read after my earthly departure. This letter will leave behind a legacy of goodwill. It may recount the special moments we shared together, offer assurance where there are doubts, or make suggestions for peace of mind. Mostly, the letter will offer a farewell message of love to lessen the grief of my beloved life partner. ℘

My Will and Other Financial Matters

I vow to draft a last will and testament with the aid of a competent attorney and to make certain that my spouse knows the location of this vital document, as well as the location of bank and investment records, life insurance policies, my social security number, income tax returns, and military records, if applicable. By putting forth this effort early, I'm ensuring that my final wishes are fulfilled and lessening the burdens of my spouse during her/his period of bereavement. ℘

The Emotions of Dying

I vow to gather strength upon my beloved's deathbed by speaking of happier memories. And in between, I'll prepare myself for the emotional stages my mate will pass through, while journeying toward the inevitable:

- ❧ Denial—*Not me, I'll be fine.*
- ❧ Fear, anger, envy, and resentment—*Why me?*
- ❧ Bargaining—*If I live, I promise to become a better person.*
- ❧ Depression—*Oh, just let me die and get it over with!*
- ❧ Acceptance—*I'm ready to pass on.*

Anticipating these stages will help me to absorb some of the sadness and confusion so that I may set my heart and mind upon sharing testaments of love with my beloved partner. ❧

Grieving

I vow to remember that the ritual of grieving is a natural healing process. The stages of grief are so universal that countless spouses share them. I'm not alone in my feelings. My grief may last for an extended period, with tears, a loss of appetite, and restless sleep. So I'll draw needed support from family and friends. But when they expect me to move on with my life, the support may wane and cause a depression filled with loneliness and withdrawal—which slows the moving-on process. But that's when I'll rely upon my glorious will to survive. I'll remember that my mate wants me as happy now as when we were together physically, and that we're forever joined spiritually. And these precious thoughts will revive my energy, my positive outlook on life, and my desire to socialize with others. ❧

Rituals of Peace
and Honor

After the physical passing of my mate, I vow to embrace avenues that encourage the cathartic act of purging, which aids in releasing distress and reaching emotional liberation. For one, the funeral service is my last public opportunity to honor my beloved's life. By presenting a testimony that celebrates fond memories of our love and life together, I'm also finding peace. Likewise, I'll write a private letter to my beloved. Within it, I'll pour out all my love, regrets, appreciation, sorrows, and memories, until I'm drained of all emotions. Then I'll plant this letter at the root of a young tree or flowering bush. And as this special memorial shrub grows, so will my life into the future. ❧

Peace

Because our deaths are inevitable, we each vow to help lessen the other's grief by following these guides for PEACE:

Prepare—I'll remain mindful that each day we have together is precious and a future memory in the making.

Eternalize—I'll remember that through life and death, our love is endless.

Accept—I'll accept the reality of death, and if needed, I'll learn more about the stages of dying and grieving.

Comfort—I'll remember that peace comes with time and spending it with loving supporters, and by recalling our happiest times together.

Endure—I'll make certain that my beloved's grief becomes peaceful by leaving behind a legacy of trust, respect, kindness, and true love. ❧

Part II

From My Contemporary Wedding Vows

Chapter 10

I Promised to Communicate

When I vowed to encourage strong communication within our union, my intentions were to ensure compatibility, fairness, and the longevity of our marriage. We can reach this goal by remembering that communication is a skill that we can always improve upon, and that communicating well is the key to a healthy marriage.

Remembering to Communicate

Sometimes it seems that the word *communicate* has become a cliché, in regard to relationships. How often is it offered as the immediate prescription for most any problem between two lovers? Yet, I now understand why. For as much as we feel we know each other, we're forging a new path as husband and wife. Our marriage is an uncharted journey fueled by the expectations, desires, fears, and insecurities of two unique individuals traveling as one. *All will be okay,* we think. *My beloved knows me and will figure out my needs.* Mind reading—what a burden to place upon anyone, especially when it's easy to speak honestly. Therefore, my dearest, I vow to remember that any expectation, desire, or insecurity that finds a place in my heart is also welcomed upon your ear. ✍

Venting Without Fear

I promise to keep quarrels in perspective. Instead of being afraid to vent my grievances, fearing that an argument might cause a breakup, I'll remember that all married couples have disagreements. In healthy marriages like ours, spouses can confess their concerns and grow closer as a result. We know how to sprinkle humor into the conversation to ease the tension. And we know the harm in character assassinations, name-calling, and unproven accusations. Therefore, I vow to vent without fear and with respect for you and our union. ✍

Handling Anger

It is essential to handle anger with care. To do otherwise could put all we've built together in jeopardy. So when necessary, we'll alert the other that we need a cooling-off period until we can both speak less vindictively. We won't stifle old grudges until we eventually explode. Rather, we'll talk out problems as they arise and until they're resolved, then put that issue to rest. When a dispute does arise, we'll be certain to deal with the *real* problem. Why complain about dirty dishes when the real anger stems from a forgotten anniversary? Lastly, we'll avoid dragging arguments out, pettiness, and bitterness. All this we vow for the sake of our precious endurance.

Words That Hinder Discussions

I now realize that our word choices determine the success or failure of our discussions. When I'm venting my frustrations and I begin sentences with *you*, I'm immediately sending feelings of blame. Anyone would become defensive. But when I use the words *I, my, me,* and *we* and share how a situation makes me feel, you're apt to listen more openly and objectively. I'll also avoid closing our talks completely by adding *never* to those blaming *you* words, for instance, *You never help around the house!* Instead, I pledge to practice a more loving and productive approach, for example, *I would feel so much better if we worked as a team on housework.* And speaking like this ensures a lifetime of further healthy discussions as husband and wife. ✌

Always Right?

I promise to examine whether I feel the need to win all debates and have the last word in all conversations with my beloved, in other words, whether I must always be right! If this is the case, I vow to be more empathetic and consider how this must make you feel. Instead of anticipating my victory, I'll suppress such urges. So, instead of thinking up my next strategic comeback, then breaking in to say it, I vow to concentrate more on what you are saying and to take your views under serious consideration. All this I vow to remember, because in the final analysis, we both should feel a sense of comfort by the conclusion of each discussion. That's how we'll make our marriage a win-win experience.

The Time and Place

I must remember that there are appropriate times and places for expressing concerns. It's unfair of me to call my beloved on the job with stormy feelings and complex issues to resolve. We should also never vent our frustrations in the presence of children, in public, or while socializing with friends or family. Doing either is extremely inconsiderate, inappropriate, and often upsetting for everyone. When there's a lack of privacy, my partner can't react as desired. Worse, we add the pressure and awkwardness of having an audience. Therefore, if angered in the presence of others or while my partner is at work, I vow to schedule a discussion for our soonest private opportunity. ❧

Lecturing

Even if I'm angered or frustrated, I vow to temper my topics with discretion and to keep my words at a minimum. Sometimes, while presenting their version of a situation, partners speak their minds in what seems like an endless monologue. This is not a discussion: it's a lecture. I'm not giving my partner a chance to respond when I do this. When I'm through and he/she finally has a chance to speak, my beloved may be so overwhelmed that points are forgotten. This creates a one-sided conversation. As partners—and not a parent or teacher to the other—we owe each other a fair chance to share opinions. ❧

Speak

When communicating with my beloved, I vow to SPEAK of my ideas, feelings, concerns, and opinions in the following manner:

Sincerely—I will always speak to you honestly and from the heart, and I'll respond with fair feedback should our discussions alter my original views.

Pointedly—I'll avoid exaggerations, drudging up past conflicts in our current conversations, and masking the true source of my anger with unrelated complaints.

Equitably—I'll listen to you intently so that my responses may assure you that you were indeed heard clearly and your thoughts are under consideration.

Articulately—Before a major discussion, if needed, I'll collect my thoughts mentally or on paper so that I'm able to convey them to you in a clear manner.

Kindly—I'll remember that everything can be said either lovingly or hostilely and that my words can be slanted either way by my attitude. Therefore, even when upset, I'll make certain that my words stem from a caring heart. ❧

Chapter 11

I Promised: The Best I Can Be

Self-esteem, reliability, flexibility, humor, and contentment are just some of the personal traits needed by both partner in order to form a solid relationship. Because I understand this, I pledged to you at our wedding to strive toward being the best I can be throughout our marriage. Today, I'll vow to put a plan into action that aids in accomplishing this important goal.

Becoming a Whole Person

Too many spouses jumped into marriage before preparing for it, before learning how to maintain strong healthy relationships by establishing them with friends and family members, and before reaching goals that are best achieved when single, with complete autonomy. Still, it's never too late. If I have goals I need to achieve that can enhance my self-esteem, therefore making me a better spouse, I'll do everything I can to achieve them. I'll also continue building close relationships with friends and family members. All of these ties develop my nurturing skills and make me a better person. I vow to ensure my wholeness as a married individual by consistently developing a full and satisfying life, realizing that this benefits both my partner and me. ৮৯

Personal Responsibility

My beloved, I vow to take my share of responsibility in developing a lasting relationship. Because I desire a happy union without lies, disrespect, and other destructive behavior, I'll start by eliminating these traits from my own character. I'll aid in keeping our home warm and comfortable by agreeing to furnishings and decorations that appeal to us both, by updating the interior periodically and making repairs when needed, and by keeping our surroundings neat and pleasant. I'll aid in keeping our finances lucrative by sticking to our planned budgets and discussing major purchases with you before buying them. I'll join in keeping our love alive by remaining desirable, flexible, a little unpredictable, and imaginative. I am now your life partner in every sense of the word. All that I expect from you, I will offer as well. ✍

Self-Doubt

Whether you, my love, and others are singing my praises, it's how I feel about myself that determines my self-worth. Sure, we all enter marriage with some degree of emotional baggage. Whether we feel proud, successful, and enthused or fearful, defeated, and dispirited is most often determined by our previous relationships and experiences, and by what we have learned, positive or negative, from those experiences. But because I vowed at our wedding to offer you my all, I now vow to do whatever it takes to escape any lingering unhealthy thoughts, until I've reached inner harmony. Only then can I truly see you, my love, as fairly as you deserve. ❧

Escaping Self-Doubts

I vow to embrace a positive attitude about myself, to feel good about myself, whether others live up to my expectations, or whether I live up to theirs. I can neither please everyone nor change anyone. So, I will encourage others and hope they also develop positive changes for themselves. I will value and celebrate the things I do well, no matter how great or small. It's okay to feel dissatisfied with myself at times; distress motivates me to learn and improve. I will listen to criticism, but objectively, keeping what helps and discarding the rest. I will surround myself only with positive people who truly care about my well-being. Finally, I will purge all of my past pains in a private written letter. Then I'll dig a hole and bury it. There, I'll say earnestly, "Ashes to ashes, dust to dust, my past is behind me, and a fresh glorious future awaits."

Maintaining My Identity

Too many partners lose their identities within the marriage. Sometimes they change by trying to be who they think the other wants. Sometimes they lose their natural spirit by succumbing to daily and yearly routines. You fell in love with and married me for who I am—for my unique style, my positive attitude, my funny little quirks. My sensitivities, sympathies, and independence fascinated you. Of course, personal growth inevitably creates changes. But those changes should enhance, not detract from, my individuality. Therefore, my beloved, I pledge to maintain the best of my individuality while adding traits that only enhance my spiritual, emotional, physical, and intellectual well-being. ✍

Self-Nurturing

Although I've grown into the role of a wife/husband, I should never neglect the people, places, and things that feed my individual spirit. My personal sources of enjoyment, fascination, and peace are life necessities. It's vital to maintain hobbies and special friendships. Quiet time and favorite sources of entertainment are essential for my peace of mind and happiness. As long as my activities respect our marriage, it's neither selfish nor inconsiderate to take "me" time. My partner and I share a world of life experiences, and it's healthy to occasionally rejuvenate apart. I vow to remember the necessity of self-nurturing, to enjoy my private times free of guilt, and to encourage and understand you when you need the same. ✑

Other Important Relationships

We need various types of personal relationships to be complete. We're not one-dimensional people. We're lovers, parents, professionals, hobby enthusiasts, friends, and family members with issues and histories. Can only one type of relationship satisfy our complex needs and interests? Of course not. Talking to an old friend who "knew me when" is like going home. There's my personal consultant, who advises me on everything from the best places to shop for antiques to finding the best greens for golf. There's the friend who offers a shoulder to cry on when the chips are down. There's the coworker or day-care parent to whom I relate so well. Yes, I vow to remember that I need a team of healthy, appropriate relationships to maintain emotional balance, and that being a good friend to others makes me a better marriage partner. ✒

A Whole Spouse

I vow to remain a whole individual throughout this marvelous marital experience by pursuing these personal goals. A spouse who is a WHOLE individual is:

Well focused—I maintain enough focus, drive, and discipline to achieve my personal goals.

Healthy—I keep my body fit by consuming nutritious meals and adequate amounts of water. I maintain a physical fitness regimen, and I have regular medical checkups.

Outgoing—I make new friends by being approachable at work and when socializing, and I communicate in a style that's civil and friendly, complimentary and gracious.

Loving—I am loving with others and also with myself. I take personal time to pamper my mind, body, and spirit by, perhaps, reading poetry by candlelight in a scented bubble bath or treating myself to spirit-lifting gifts, or savoring "me time" on a mountaintop.

Embracing—I develop a zest for life by maintaining a wide range of interests and a healthy adventurous spirit or by learning more about the cultures and traditions of those with whom I share the world.

Chapter 12

❧❧❧❧❧❧❧

I Promised to Make Your Family My Own

When entering into the sublime state of matrimony,
I'm establishing an eternal bond not only with my
new mate but also with my beloved's family. My hope
is to help create a melting pot in which we all can
share, nurture, and love one another for a lifetime.

In-laws

I will never choose "tolerating" my in-laws over "enjoying" them. Although there may be times when I disagree with their behavior or advice, I'll keep in mind that they sincerely love the same person I love and married. I'll remember that they raised my beloved and guided him/her to my heart. Therefore, I vow to relax if feeling intimidated by them, to speak my mind respectfully and with the best of intentions, and to always honor the blessing of these extended family members. ❧

Stepchildren

Families with shared bloodlines have difficulties, so why should stepfamilies be any easier? Fear of the unknown and changes are common when single parents marry and form a new unit. Some get along fine. Others have issues. Perhaps the remarriage created extra sets of parents, in-laws, and siblings. Maybe the children must adjust to a new home, friends, and me. Initially, they may not accept their stepsiblings, or me as an authority figure. To achieve a congenial family unit, I vow to take these vital steps: Instead of being caught off-guard, I'll anticipate potential challenges based on the varied personalities and, as always, discuss workable strategies with my mate. We'll establish a chain of command early and communicate clearly to the children. I won't rush the development of relationships. And I'll maintain the belief that patience, diplomacy, empathy, respect, and caring reap victorious results.

Ex-spouses

Bad blood is practically a tradition within our society between ex-spouses and new spouses. Ex-wives and ex-husbands sometimes view the new mates as their replacement. Likewise, when shared children are involved, new mates occasionally feel threatened by the ongoing ties of the ex. Throw in the drama that often prevails between spouses and their exs and the blend can be anything but cohesive. It's time we break this destructive mold and progress from the dysfunctional family mentality. Unless the ex is an extreme burden upon the new marriage, there's no reason we can't grant each other respectful courtesies. And when the parent in the middle inspires unity between the ex and the new mate, it benefits everyone's future, especially the children's. Therefore, regardless of relationship histories, I vow to break tradition and offer the ex the same civility, respect, and inclusion I would give to any extended family member. ❧

Multicultural Family Members

Because we're living in an age when diverse cultures mingle more than ever, it's not uncommon that our blended families include the same diversity. Some family members may live in the country, others in the city. Some embrace classical music; others prefer rap. And to further spice up life, today's glorious families may include a variety of racial, ethnic, and religious members. Of course, no group is inferior; they're simply different. The best way to ensure cohesiveness is by appreciating both the differences and similarities. There's much to learn and share within the intimacy of families that broadens everyone's outlook. We can visit new places, try unfamiliar foods, and explore intriguing new customs. Therefore, I vow to view myself as fortunate to gain a wealth of multicultural family members. I will certainly expand my world by relaxing and enjoying the fascinating variety among my family. ❦

Extended Family

Although our union is blissful and feels complete, we are not in this world alone. We are products of family members who shared in all the years of our development. Parents, aunts, uncles, cousins, sisters, brothers, and even close family friends care about the longevity of our union. They care about each of us individually. They want to remain in our lives. We can turn to these extended family members when answers to unforeseen challenges escape us. We should inform them of and invite them to share in our small and grand celebrations. Together, we make one another's lives more complete. This is why I vow to honor our wealth of extended family members, and to ensure that they are all happily and securely a part of our lives. ๛

Developing
Family Ties

I vow to strive toward cohesive relationships with my new family members. And I create FAMILY feelings by being:

Familiar—I treat family like friends and make them feel welcome when visiting my home.

Affectionate—I offer hugs, kisses, and loving, heartfelt words.

Mindful—I record everyone's birthdays and anniversaries and share in their observances.

Interested—I show interest in my in-law's topics of conversation and prized possessions. I initiate chats that inspire them to share more about themselves.

Leisurely—I make the best impression by being relaxed and myself at all times.

Yielding—I offer tactful and diplomatic advice or opinions upon request.

Chapter 13

I Promised to Keep Our Marriage Alive

As the marriage unfolds, regardless of pledging to do otherwise, too often spouses relax some of the wondrous attributes that inspired the earlier wedding bells. Thus I'm eager to master the arts of creative and limitless thinking.

Marriage by Design

There are so many misconceptions about marriage. Some have jokingly called a spouse the old ball and chain and have even called marriage a prison. I have to laugh, because people with these attitudes completely miss the real point of marriage. Marriage is what we make it. Our union should be a kaleidoscope of all the life experiences we cherish and enjoy, need and desire. As long as our choices honor our wedding vows, the sky's the limit! Why fall into the slump of predictable ruts? We have a wealth of small and great choices to make for the rest of our lives. Happily, I pledge to join you in spreading our wings and flying through the freshness of unforeseen tomorrows.

Comfort Zones

It's said that when you pour goldfish from a small bowl into a larger one, the fish still swim within the small amount of space they had before. Many married couples aren't much different. We find our comfort zones within an established lifestyle that is filled with routine habits that we share with people in our community. While comfort and security are important, we owe it to ourselves to break free of stagnation and fly forth and beyond the familiar. Therefore, I vow to venture beyond the norm and start new family traditions. Perhaps we'll take classes together to learn fun skills such as Japanese cooking or oil painting, or we can buy mountain bikes and explore unfamiliar trails. We can turn strangers into friends by joining travel clubs, church groups, and civic organizations as a couple. And we can change our daily routines by simply deciding to alter our predictable ways with fun and romantic twists. After all, expanding our comfort zone enriches the quality of our relationship. &

Playfulness

I admire couples who tease each other unmercifully, even in public, yet neither takes offense. When spouses are able to laugh at each other's quirks, they exude feelings of being completely certain of the other's affections. Each is so secure with his or her strengths and weaknesses that a little ribbing is simply playful. And let's not forget to share all of the whimsical joys that make us feel light and carefree, such as rolling down grassy hills and building snowmen. We should let a giant roller coaster take our breath away, then giggle about it over twirls of cotton candy. Why not start pillow fights when least expected, tickle each other, or dress up for Halloween and trick-or-treat at the homes of friends and family? Because laughter keeps a relationship sparkling and alive, I vow to enhance and celebrate the playful spirit within us both. ❧

Spontaneous Public Affection

Who said that you can't treat your spouse like a cherished date in public? Marriage doesn't make us suddenly uptight. We should still enjoy throwing our cares to the wind and romancing whenever inspired. Spontaneity is our marital spice. Impulsiveness adds zest to any outing. Buying flowers on impulse from a street vendor is a great way to share my joy with you. Or I might propose marriage to you all over again, after buying a candy or toy ring along the way. A little cuddling, smooching, and playfulness in public are a fantastic recipe for our eternal love affair. Just as I appreciate shows of adoration, if my mate and I are inspired, I vow to free myself from any inhibitions that rob our relationship of spontaneous affection. ❧

Enjoying Each Day

I vow to make the most of each day. Something as simple as adding flowers to the dinner table or making fun fashion statements elevates our spirits. We feel good when we offer each other a gift for no apparent reason. Life's also exciting when we plan exotic trips and pleasant outings. Amazing museums, hot-air balloon rides, street festivals, picnics in the park—they're all waiting for our enjoyment. And whether it's a birthday, an anniversary, a holiday celebration, or no particular occasion at all, throwing parties is lots of fun, and it adds luster to our relationship. Today is ours to love and live completely. Why hoard all the money we work so hard for or put off having fun until sometime in the future? Let's embrace life with gusto and make memories every day. ❧

Make Together-Time

Life's obligations often minimize the precious time we plan together. Between our separate careers, hobbies, interests, and commitments, we find ourselves dreaming of "someday," that elusive time together when the kids are older or our careers finally take off. Why wait? To reverse this trend, I vow to negotiate shared time that not only accommodates our personal interests but also creates a feeling of togetherness when we're apart. We can do this by setting aside "our time" in between personal activities. Instead of criticizing each other's interests, we'll learn the value of sharing them. We might record our feelings and ideas in a daily journal, then exchange them like love notes, and e-mail each other romantic messages at work. And when we clip articles and jot down jokes to pass on to each other, we're conveying this message: *I was thinking about you.* Time together, whether near or far, can be a joyous reality. ♨

Alive

We pledge to help keep our loving marriage FRESH and alive by remembering these helpful hints:

Fun—All work and no play deprives our spirits of cheery sensations from fireworks, Ferris wheels, pillow fights, and all other inspiring marital moments of joy.

Relaxation—I'll release the baggage, if any, and enjoy receiving happiness, great surprises, and loving treatment from my mate that is so wonderful that reciprocating comes easily.

Energy—New sparks ignite when we update the appeal of ourselves and home, add creative ideas to our intimacy, and take delight in fresh areas of interest.

Spontaneity—Ditch the itineraries and discover rainbows, and seashells, and waterfalls, and paradise on a moment's notice.

Heart—The heart of marital liveliness is having the heart to keep my beloved amazed, curious, spirited, and wholesome for the rest of our lives as one.